*This book is dedicated to all who find Nature not an adversary to conquer and destroy, but a storehouse of infinite knowledge and experience linking man to all things past and present. They know conserving the natural environment is essential to our future well-being.*

# BISCAYNE
## THE STORY BEHIND THE SCENERY®

### by L. Wayne Landrum

Wayne Landrum, chief ranger at Biscayne National Park, has worked in parks from coast to coast since starting his National Park Service career at Carlsbad Caverns National Park. A native of New Mexico, he holds a degree in biology from Southern Utah State University. Wayne's many years of living in these unique preserves has deepened his appreciation of America's natural wonders.

**Biscayne National Park,** located off the southeastern coast of Florida, set aside in 1968, protects islands, water, coral reefs, plants, animals, and marine life.

Front cover: Snorkelers view fish among the corals, photo by Stephen Frink. Inside front cover: Photographing the laughing gulls, photo by Rob Simpson. Title page: Squirrelfish, photo by Stephen Frink. Pages 2/3: Sunrise over Biscayne, photo by James A. Kern.

Edited by Mary L. Van Camp. Book design by K. C. DenDooven.

First Printing, 1990

BISCAYNE: THE STORY BEHIND THE SCENERY © 1990, KC PUBLICATIONS, INC.
LC 90-61963. ISBN 0-88714-048-3.

**T**he sun rises in the park bringing warmth and light.
This is a place of life; from the sea and from the land.
It is a place of natural beauty with flowing colors,
brightly painted fish, birds, and other tropical creatures—
a wild place that draws us back to the sea.

*Biscayne National Park was established as a national monument in 1968, then expanded to a national park in 1980. Biscayne Bay was probably named by Spanish explorers for the Bay of Biscay, between Spain and France or, as one legend has it, for a Spaniard named Vixcayno held prisoner in the Florida Keys. The coastal boundary provides a buffer between the greater Miami area and the park. Water is the highway into the area and several hundred thousand people come by powerboats, sailboats, and charter boats every year. They come to see the natural beauty of the park, brightly colored fish, the reefs that dot the shallow waters, and to escape the noise and crowds of the city.*

Boca Chita Key with its beautiful harbor and lighthouse is an attraction for boaters and sightseers.

*Biscayne Bay, a large, shallow sea
of emerald-green water
located almost entirely within the park boundaries,
is alive with sea creatures such as
the spiny lobster, sponges, fish, and soft corals.*

# A Place on the Edge

A place on the edge—Biscayne National Park begins where the continent ends! This 181,500-acre marine park at the southeast tip of the United States is perched on the continental shelf—bordered on the one side by the East Coast and dropping into the Atlantic Ocean on the edge of the Gulf Stream on the other side.

It is a combination of green coastal wetlands; clear, shallow seas; barrier islands; and beautiful reefs—all different, but related, and all supporting an abundance of life both in and out of the water. The water is warm and the year-round climate subtropical.

The park starts just south of Miami on the coast and follows the mainland south to the end of Biscayne Bay at Card Sound. This 26-mile boundary is an area composed primarily of wetlands, where fresh water meets the salt water of the sea and the types of vegetation and animals change from freshwater to saltwater species.

Coastal vegetation is dominated by salt-tolerant trees called mangroves. They provide a buffer for the park from one of the fastest developing communities in the United States.

Biscayne Bay, a large, shallow sea of emerald-green water located almost entirely within the park boundaries, is alive with sea creatures such as the spiny lobster, sponges, fish, and soft corals. The bay averages five feet deep, rarely exceeding ten feet. The bay bottom has life-supporting beds of turtle grass and algae. Boating across this crystal-clear water is an exhilarating experience with the underwater life in full view.

◀ **Sailing on Biscayne Bay is a popular** *attraction because of its usually gentle winds, warm water, and mild climate.*

**Within Biscayne National Park is the** ▶ *northern extension of the Florida Keys. These islands are the remains of coral reefs that have been left exposed to the air as the sea level dropped over many thousands of years. Covered with a tangled mass of vegetation, these green islands provide shelter to many of the park's birds and animals.*

> *Where the sea meets the islands, mangroves and buttonwood trees fringe the water's edge. Inland, hardwood hammocks grow, with lush exotic plants and trees.*

On the east side of Biscayne Bay, several miles off the coast, lie the barrier islands. These are the northernmost islands of the Florida Keys, a narrow chain of ancient, exposed coral reefs, 150 miles long. "Key" is a term from the Spanish word *cayo*, which means "islet," or small island.

There are 32 islands inside the park totaling about 7,000 acres. They are very low, rarely exceeding an elevation of 8 feet above sea level. Dense tropical and subtropical vegetation covers them. Where the sea meets the islands, mangroves and buttonwood trees fringe the water's edge, with thousands of roots seeking toeholds in the silt. Inland, hardwood hammocks grow, with lush exotic plants and trees. These hardwood trees tower over the mangroves.

Birds are common in and around the islands. Brown pelicans, cormorants, frigate birds, blue herons, snowy egrets, and other fishing birds are common sights. Only a few species of mammals live on the islands: raccoons, rabbits, squirrels, and mice make their homes there. Several species of reptiles are found including the eastern diamond back rattlesnake. During the summer months, the air is thick with the most common animal to inhabit the islands—the mosquito.

This chain of barrier islands is broken by creeks. They connect the waters of Biscayne Bay with the Atlantic to the east, thus providing passages between the islands to open water. Used by man for hundreds of years, modern-day boaters use these "cuts" to gain access to the deeper waters of the Atlantic and the Gulf Stream. There are no roads or bridges connecting the islands to the mainland or to the rest of the Florida Keys. Public access is by boat only. The islands are mostly undeveloped, but have an exciting history of habitation by Indians, explorers, pirates, wreckers, farmers, and developers.

Beyond the low islands, a narrow shelf extends below the surface of the water for several miles before dropping rapidly into the deep blue Atlantic Ocean. The park extends to a depth of 60 feet on its eastern boundary on the edge of the fast-moving Gulf Stream. The Gulf Stream brings warm water into the park and is a necessary ingredient for reef-building coral. Coral has to have water warmer than 68 degrees in order to survive. Bright sunny days and clear water containing nutrients are available here at this southeastern corner of the United States where coral reefs are formed.

The conditions are just right for the reefs to grow, and they are the most unique and exciting features of the park. Teeming with life, the coral reefs are a dynamic force of nature. As the organisms live and die, their skeletons form rock that continually builds, reaching for the sunshine from the water.

The reefs attract thousands of people each year who explore the exciting life below the sea by boat, scuba, and snorkel.

### SUGGESTED READING

GILBREATH, ALICE. *River in the Ocean.* Minneapolis, Minnesota: Dillon Press, Inc., 1986.

ORR, KATHERINE. *The Wondrous World of the Mangrove Swamps.* Miami, Florida: Florida Flair Books, 1989.

🔺 **Buttonwood trees grow just above the high-tide level.** These trees, like mangroves, are salt tolerant but do not grow in the intertidal zone constantly exposed to flooding. They grow on more solid ground. The vegetation must adapt to a very shallow soil cover in this area. The exposed limestone here is "oolite," the common rock of the mainland. It is jagged, sharp, and hard to walk on.

◀ **Mangrove trees fringe the coastal areas and islands.** These trees grow in salt water. The red is the most common of three types of mangroves, and is easily recognized by its branching prop roots. This tree stabilizes the shoreline and provides shelter for animals living in the intertidal zone.

🔺 **Land crabs live in the wet mangrove swamps.** These animals dig holes in the mud above the high-tide mark and forage for food near the water's edge. Once common in south Florida, they are now found in large numbers only in protected areas where their habitat has not been destroyed.

**Porkfish prefer the shallow** waters. These beautiful fish swim in schools for protection, making it harder on predators to single out any one fish. Porkfish are recognized by the vertical black and white stripes on the head and behind the gill. These fish usually feed at night on worms, mollusks, and brittle stars. They average about a foot in length.

◀ **Brown pelicans are found on** the East and West coasts. These large birds feed on fish by diving into the water from as high as 30 feet in the air. The birds catch fish in their mouth, which has a large pouch. Pelicans are graceful flyers, often gliding just above the water.

▲ **Biscayne National Park is a water park with 95 percent of its surface covered with water.** *Conditions are perfect for the coral reefs which are dynamic, living communities with a multitude of tenants—each dependent on the other. People are visitors to this underwater world, either diving or snorkeling. The smooth trunkfish seems entranced by the visitor. This small fish searches the bottom for food and can blow a powerful jet of water from its mouth to uncover edible animals in the sand.*

*One hundred thousand years ago the sea level here was 25 feet higher than it is today, with all of south Florida under water. Two types of limestone developed —Miami and Key Largo.*

# Water and Rock

All of south Florida is flat. The coastal ridge is the highest land along the eastern side of the state. This ridge extends from Georgia to south Florida near Homestead. It reaches its highest point of 20 feet above sea level at Coconut Grove. This is the highest natural point in all of south Florida.

Over the years the sea level constantly rises and falls. During cold periods, the polar ice caps increase in size, locking up water from the planet and causing a drop in sea level. During warm periods, water is released as the ice melts and the level of the sea rises.

One hundred thousand years ago the sea level here was 25 feet higher than it is today, with all of south Florida under water. In the marine environment that existed at the time, two types of limestone developed—Miami and Key Largo—some of the youngest in the United States.

The Miami Limestone, covering all of south Florida except the Florida Keys, was deposited by marine organisms that secreted or produced calcium carbonate (limestone) during their life cycle. Some of the building material was *ooids* (loose sand grains) that settled to the bottom, and some was created by animals such as *Bryozoans* (small invertebrate animals that lived in colonies), sea

◀ **Limestone is the** foundation for south Florida and the Florida Keys. This limestone is some of the most recent rock to form in the United States. As the sea level dropped, the sedimentary rock was left above the surface. Plants such as the saltwort began to grow, starting the cycle where debris builds up to begin the routine of soil building and preventing erosion.

*The Florida Keys, including the 32 islands of Biscayne, were once under water. Old Rhodes Key is one of these islands that developed as living coral reefs, building up large limestone foundations over time. As the sea receded and was exposed to air, the marine life died or moved on. The process of building limestone is still going on under the sea as living corals continue to form reefs.*

worms, and other calcium-producing organisms.

At the same time, a different process was going on to the east, also in the sea. Coral reefs of limestone rock were being formed from the bottom to the surface of the sea by many different types of coral animals. This type of reef formation from coral-producing animals is called the Key Largo Limestone.

Over the eons as the climate became colder, the polar caps increased in size locking up more land and more sea water, causing a drop in the sea to its present level. As the limestone became exposed to air and rain it solidified and hardened to become the bedrock of today.

### Coral Reefs

Biscayne National Park contains the northernmost living coral reefs in the continental United States. This subtropical area, fed by the warm waters of the Gulf Stream, provides all the necessary ingredients required for a reef to live. Bright sunny days, warm clear water, and the correct salinity of the water are necessary for coral reefs to form. Just a few miles north, conditions change and the reefs do not grow.

Its open expanse of water with endless vistas, often of spectacular cloud formations and beautiful sunrises and sunsets, offers visitors to Biscayne National Park a unique experience. Most of the life of Biscayne, however, lies underwater and the reefs are a primary source of the park's beauty.

Both hard and soft corals play an important role in the ecology of the park. There are about 50 species of coral in Biscayne formed by small, barrel-

*Polyps form in colonies on the surface of limestone built up by previous generations. These living polyps in the outer layer secrete calcium carbonate and build up into massive coral heads and forms.*

shaped animals called *polyps*. These polyps attach themselves to the sea bottom, with an open mouth on top, surrounded by tentacles which contain stinging cells called "nematocysts." The cells are used for defense and for paralyzing prey.

Hard coral polyps have tentacles in multiples of six encircling their mouths. These hard corals are the rigid builders of the reef. Soft corals grow on flexible stalks, moving with the currents. They come in a variety of shapes and forms.

Polyps form in colonies on the surface of limestone built up by previous generations. These living polyps in the outer layer secrete calcium carbonate. They continue to build up limestone, layer after layer, forming massive coral heads. During the day, most hard-coral animals are not obvious because they contract and withdraw their tentacles into receptacles in the coral. It is at night, when they extend their tentacles and wave them slowly in the water to feed, that they are most easily observed.

### Hard and Soft Corals

Hard corals provide the foundation for the reefs, and contain algae living within their body tissue. These single-celled plants help the coral use up carbon dioxide which is a waste product of the polyp. Algae gives off oxygen as a product of photosynthesis, which is used by the coral. It acts as a catalyst in the production of limestone, thus assisting the growth of the coral reef. These algae are called *zooxanthellae*, and the relationship is beneficial to both the corals and the algae. Common hard corals in Biscayne are star, elkhorn, staghorn, and brain coral.

Soft corals form living communities of polyps. They are identified by having eight tentacles. These corals form branching colonies and are often confused with plants. They are flexible and orient themselves in the current to get the best feeding position. Unlike hard corals, these often feed in the daytime and, with their tentacles exposed, have a feathery appearance. Common soft corals in the reefs are sea whips, sea feathers, sea plumes, and sea fans. Both hard and soft corals feed on plankton and organic material.

▲ **Off the Florida coast the hard and** soft corals provide protective shelter for many species of fish. The blue tang, which grows to a foot in length, is common on the corals, feeding on the abundant algae associated with the reef. This fish has a concealed lancelike spine in its tail that can cause injury to attacking fish.

**Diving beneath the surface on the reefs** ▷ reveals a fascinating variety of corals, often named for their similar appearance to common forms above the water. Brain corals are massive, grooved and circular hard corals. The staghorn is named for its resemblance to deer antlers. Sea fans and stinging coral are also found in the clear, warm waters.

## THE OUTER REEFS

The outer reef tract of Biscayne is east of the barrier islands. The patch reefs appear inside the outer reef tract, and are located in fairly protected areas. The dominant features of the patch reefs are the boulder-shaped star coral heads and brain corals. There are many soft corals such as sea fans and sea whips.

These reefs, with their many hollow spaces and hiding places, are home and shelter to many hundreds of plants and animals, including gorgeous reef fish such as the colorful parrotfish, white grunt, yellowtail snapper, damselfish, and angelfish. Other animals common here are sponges, lobsters, crabs, eels, urchins, and shrimp.

This community of plants and animals has day and night shifts. Some of the fish and crustaceans feed at night and seek protection during the day in crevices and under ledges. Daytime feeders go into hiding during the night. Many of the fish and urchins forage on nearby sea grasses, but stay close to the reef so they can escape from the predators that feed on them. Often, as a result of this local grazing, the patch reef is surrounded by a bare area of sand called a "halo."

The outer reefs are dynamic, exposed to stronger currents and wave action, and having a more diverse structure. The easternmost part of the reef drops into deeper water—this is called the "fore" reef. It is composed of large coral heads

*A greater variety of habitat is found in these outer reefs. More nomadic animals move through this area due to its location near the Gulf Stream and deeper water.*

which give it some protection from waves and storms. Elkhorn coral is common near the surface, or reef crest, along with soft corals such as sea fans and coral rubble.

The more protected "back" reef has staghorn and star corals as well as soft corals. Usually this area has a lot of coral rubble collected from storms and wave action from the wave crest. Sea grass begins to appear here and farther back thick beds of turtle grass begin to grow.

A greater variety of habitat is found in these outer reefs and more animals use them. Some of the animals found here are parrotfish, triggerfish, rock beauties, yellowtail snapper, angelfish, octopus, hogfish, sponges, and eels. More nomadic animals move through this area due to its location near the Gulf Stream and deeper water. Sea turtles, sharks (hammerhead, nurse, and blacktipped), rays, and barracuda are fairly common. Some animals pose a threat to divers and swimmers. Barracuda and sharks rarely bother divers unless they are spearing fish.

The Portuguese man-of-war is the most common animal to avoid when swimming or diving. Easily recognized by its beautifully colored gas-filled float, it floats on the surface with its tentacles hanging down into the water. On contact with prey its tentacles can deliver powerful stings. These are very painful to humans and can cause a severe reaction with some. Persons who have been stung should seek medical help immediately.

The loggerhead turtle frequents the area in its migrations. This magnificent creature may weigh 400 pounds or more. Green turtles have also been reported in the park. Sadly, many turtles are killed each year by motorboats.

## SUGGESTED READING

HUMANN, PAUL. *Reef Creatures*. Miami, Florida: University of Miami Press, 1974.

KAPLAN, EUGENE. *A Field Guide to Coral Reefs of the Caribbean and Florida*. Boston, Massachusetts: Houghton Mifflin Company, 1982.

SEFTON, NANCY and STEVEN K. WEBSTER. *A Field Guide to Caribbean Reef Invertebrates*. Monterey, California: E. J. Brill Leiden, 1986.

VOSS, GILBERT. *Coral Reefs of Florida*. Sarasota, Florida: Pineapple Press, 1988.

▲ **Some animals of the reef pose a** threat to humans. The most commonly encountered is the Portuguese man-of-war which floats through the water, powered by the wind. This gas-filled float trails long tentacles with stinging cells which can inflict painful stings to the unwary diver or snorkeler. Wet suits give some protection against this stinging, floating colony.

**Diving beneath the surface to** ▷ photograph the life under the sea is an exciting adventure of discovery. The sea fan, waving in the current, is one of the beautiful soft corals. Plantlike in appearance, it actually is composed of a colony of tiny, living animals on a flexible stalk. These sea fans position themselves in the current to take advantage of their floating food—plankton. Diving is best done with the buddy system, and here the butterfly fish looks on.

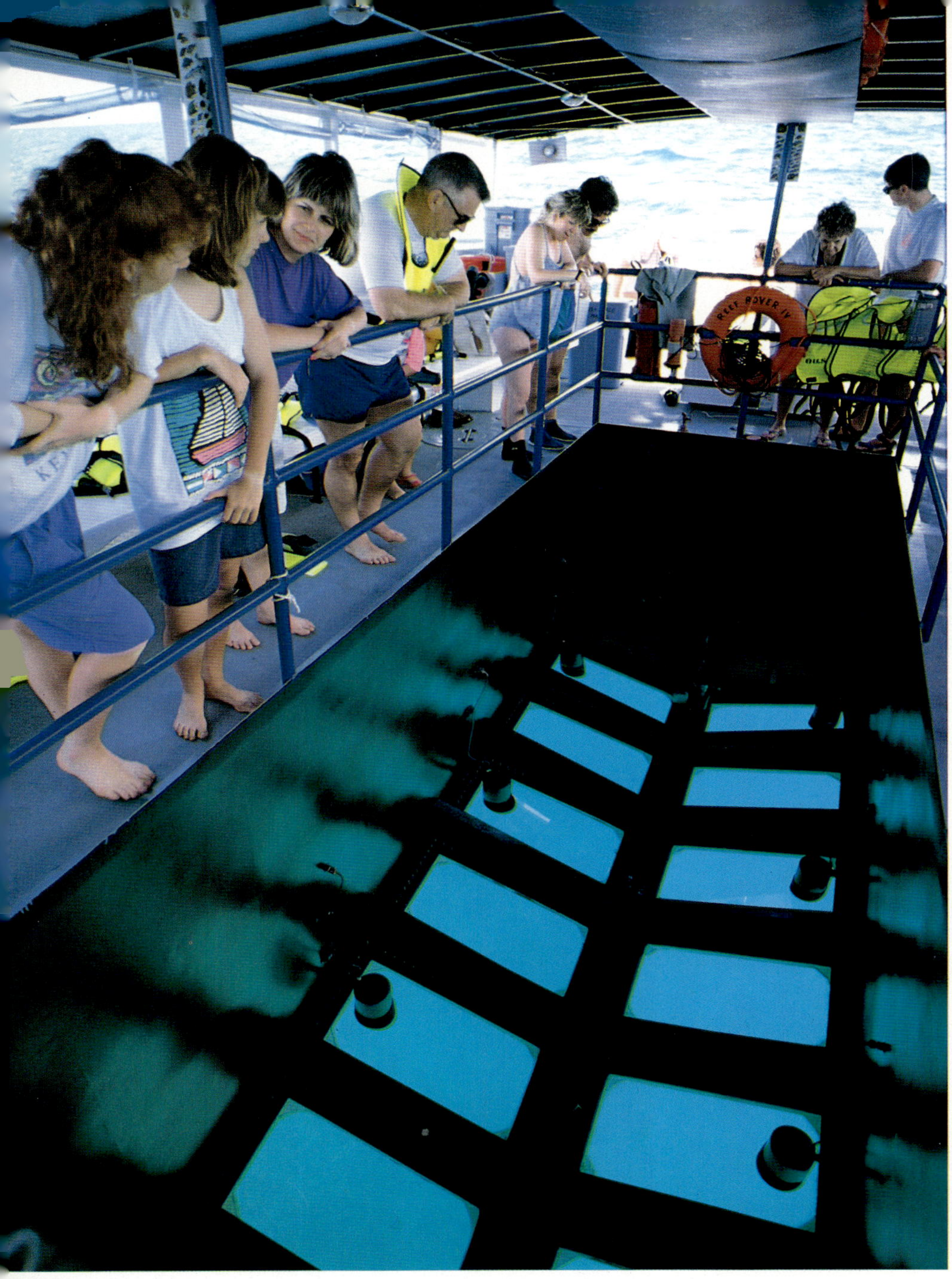

STEPHEN FRINK

STEPHEN FRINK

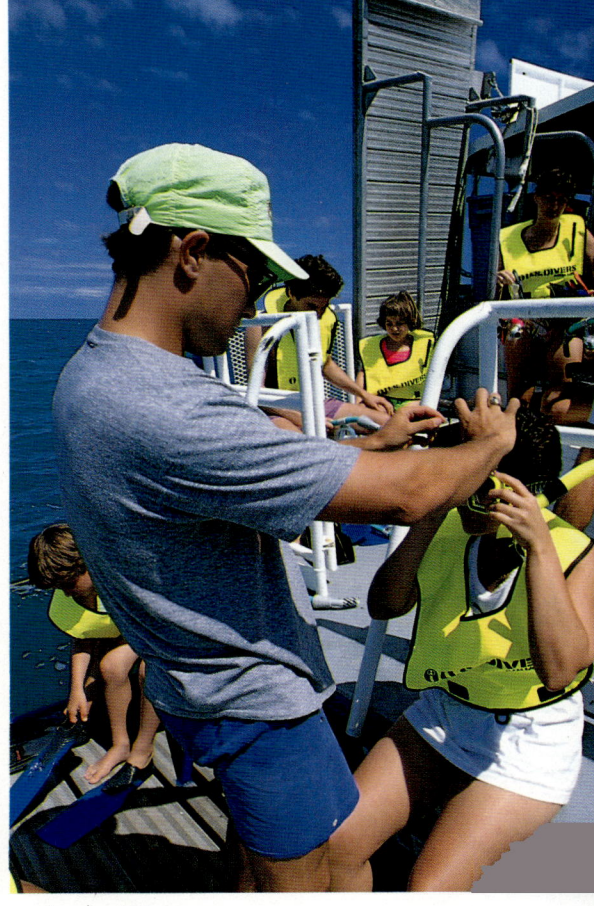

◀ ▲ ***The park has concession-*** *operated tour boats. These glass-bottom boats take visitors from the headquarters area far out into the park. Here they can view the underwater coral reefs and wildlife without getting wet. Enroute to the reefs, the boats pass through the narrow channels between the tree-covered islands. Dive and snorkel trips are also popular.*

STEPHEN FRINK

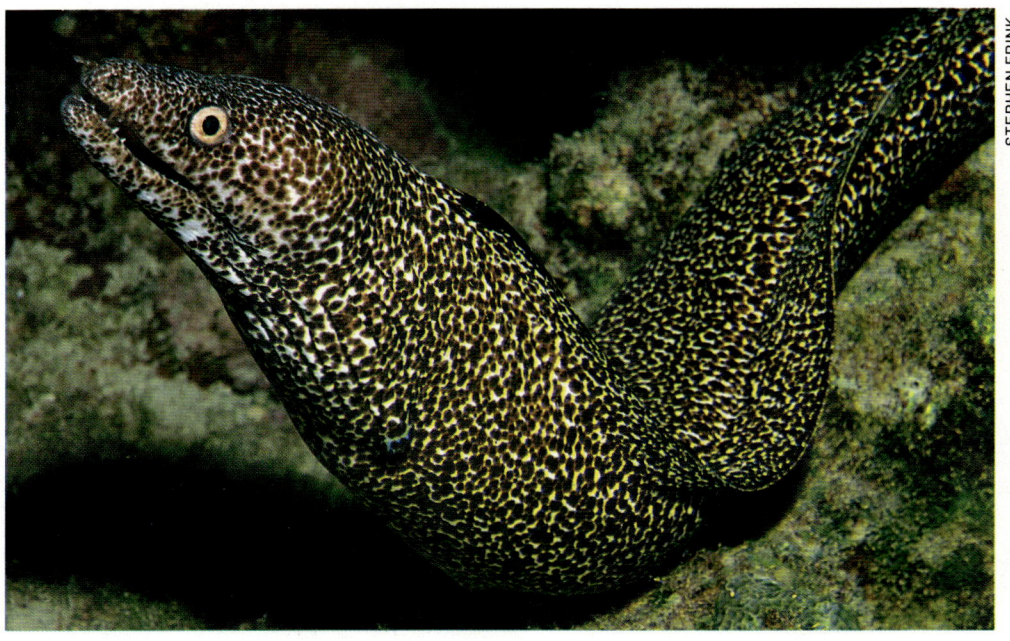

◀ ***The spotted moray is a*** *fish with the appearance of a snake. It can inflict a painful bite if disturbed or startled by someone poking through the crevices or under ledges. The eels live in crevices and feed on unsuspecting fish. They are nocturnal and are rarely encountered, preferring to be left alone.*

**There are several** species of angelfish in the park, including the grey. These fish are beautiful in color and very curious. They are popular attractions for photographers.

◄ **The spiny lobster of** Florida is closely related to the freshwater crawfish, but unlike the Maine lobster it has long antennae and no pinchers. It is protected in Biscayne Bay.

◀ **The loggerhead is the** most common turtle seen in the park. They weigh 300 to 400 pounds and have been recorded at 900 pounds. It wasn't until their numbers dropped at an alarming rate that they became protected from poachers in the late 1960s. These animals were here when the dinosaurs roamed the earth—it would be a great loss to have them disappear now!

**The reefs** ▶ provide shelter and hiding places for fish such as the beautiful blue-striped grunts. They seldom venture far away from the protective coral during the day. At night they move out away from the reef to graze in the grass flats. Elkhorn coral is common on the reefs.

20

▲ **Sharks are often a concern when diving, swimming, or snorkeling in the oceans. The bull** shark is one of the most common species in the park, but is rarely seen. Shark attacks are unusual and usually associated with spearfishing when the blood of the fish attracts them to the scene. While sharks are unpredictable, attacks are very rare.

▲ **The southern stingray glides through the** water in search of food. Stingrays normally eat bottom-dwelling animals such as crabs, clams, worms, and small fish. They usually avoid people.

◀ **Barracuda are stalkers of fish, but do not** attack humans unless provoked or attracted by a shiny object, such as a belt buckle or ring. A six-foot barracuda with its mouth full of sharp teeth can be a startling experience.

STEPHEN FRINK

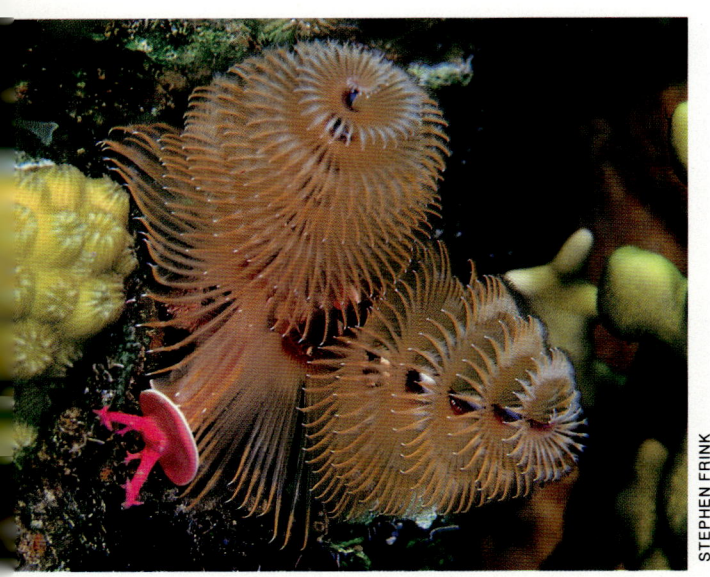

▲ **Christmas tree worms are** *some of the most colorful animals of the reef. They live embedded in the coral with their feathery gills exposed. When approached, these small animals retract rapidly into their tubes.*

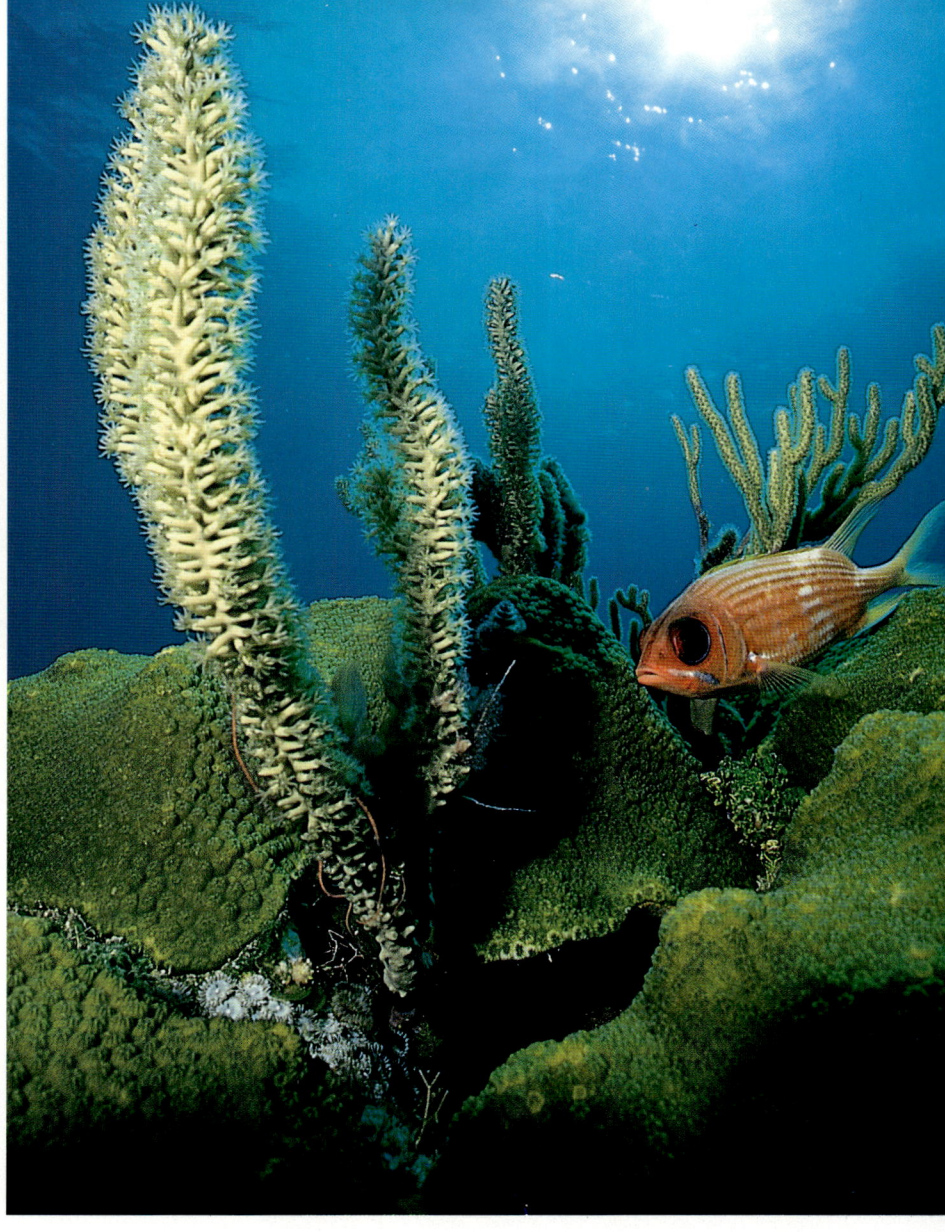

**The squirrelfish, with its large** ▶ *eye and deeply forked tail, usually comes out to feed at night on crabs and shrimp.*

STEPHEN FRINK

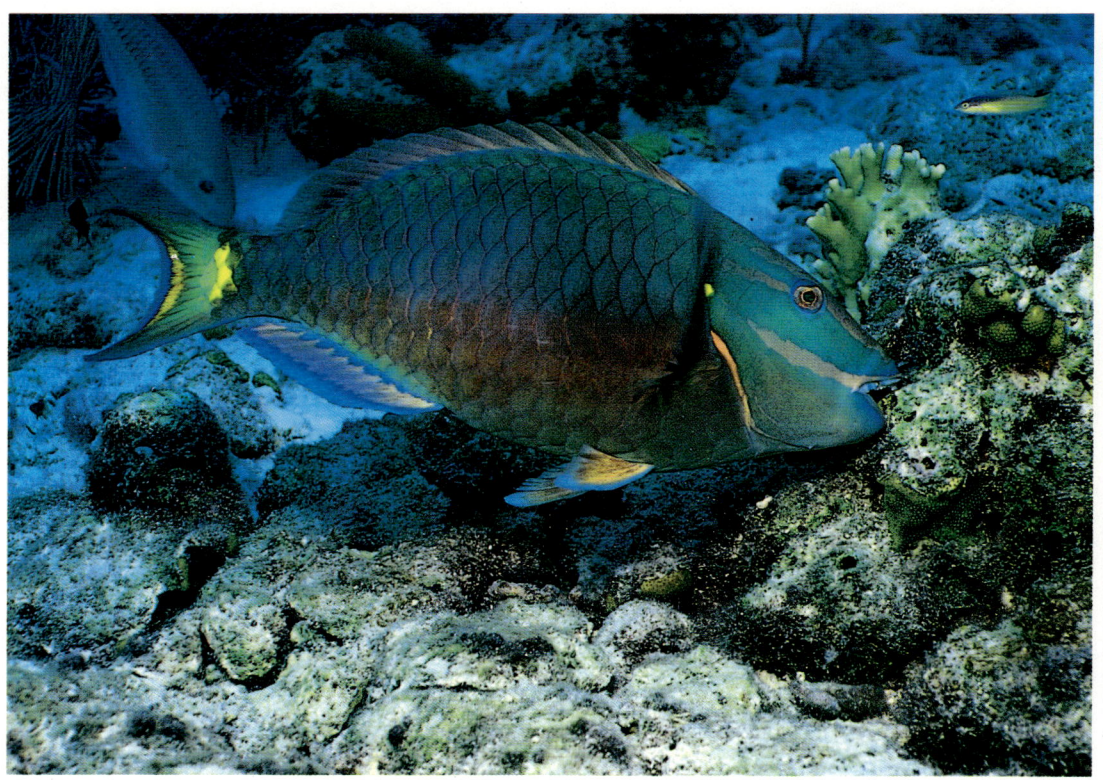

◀ **Parrotfish are** *common on the coral reefs. These colorful fish are equipped with powerful jaws and sharp teeth which allow them to chew up the hard coral and eat the algae embedded in it. They are all born female, but some dominant ones change sex to male when they mature.*

▲ **The** reefs of the park are in shallow water. These exciting animal and plant communities are easily observed by swimming on the surface or diving into the water for a closer look. Coral reefs require clean, clear, warm water. Water temperature often reaches into the 80s.

**O**verleaf: Elkhorn coral ▷ grows just under the surface of the water. Photo by Stephen Frink.

*In this area of torrential rain
and blinding thunderstorms,
the long, narrow islands are covered with green.
The trees are a welcome invitation
to birds of all kinds.*

## Islands and Shorelines

Beyond the islands and shorelines of the park, the coral reefs support large numbers of plants and animals. Vividly painted fishes and soft corals inhabit these underwater paradises. All this life under the sea is dependent to some degree on the nearby coastal area and islands.

On the shore in this subtropical environment grow an abundance of plants. Above the high-tide level are the hardwood hammocks where the trees are mostly tropical, also commonly found in the West Indies. Some of these are the gumbo limbo, Jamaican dogwood, mahogany, coconut palm, poisonwood, strangler fig, and torchwood—exotic names in an exotic environment.

In the intertidal zone where the salt water invades the land daily and then retreats again, are the most important trees of the park and for all of coastal Florida. These are the mangroves that live and grow in salt water and salt marshes, and form a buffer between the land and sea.

In this area of torrential rain and blinding thunderstorms, the long, narrow islands are covered with green. The trees are a welcome invitation to birds of all kinds.

◀ *In between the islands and crowded by mangroves are the "cuts" connecting the ocean side of the islands to Biscayne Bay. These clear-water channels are popular places to visit, especially on windy days when they provide protection from the waves. Canoes are an excellent means of transportation along the mangrove-covered shorelines.*

**During the summer rainy season this** subtropical area is a place of intense thunderstorms and rain. The area gets an average of 58 inches of rainfall each year, nourishing the green jungle on the islands. Almost daily during the summer afternoons the billowing cloud forms build up, bringing rain and thunderstorms.

The red mangrove dominates the salty waters on the sea's edge. It is easily identified by its long and slender "prop roots," hanging from the trunk and branches and growing into the water giving the tree a solid hold against the incoming waves and storms. The white and black mangroves grow back a little from the red mangroves in the higher marsh areas.

The American crocodile inhabits the estuaries along the shore and islands and may now be in the more remote locations. The crocodile prefers salt and brackish water, while the nearby alligator prefers fresh water.

The tropical forest of the park provides habitat for many species of birds. The wading birds such as the ibises, herons, egrets, bitterns, and spoonbills feed in the mangrove-lined pools and nest in the trees. Many other birds are dependent on these trees and ground cover. Often seen along the shore and in the water are brown pelicans and cormorants and, occasionally, anhingas. Ducks and loons are common as well as the high-flying frigate birds and an occasional bald eagle. In the tree canopy are hawks, falcons, vultures, and owls. Wood storks are in the area, and an occasional sighting of a peregrine falcon is reported.

There are few land mammals on the islands—raccoon, rabbits, squirrels, and mice. In the recent past other mammals, such as the white-tailed deer and bobcat, were present.

*T*he manatee is an endangered species with an estimated total population of 1,200 in Florida. The biggest threat to their safety is the powerboat.

Manatee are found in the park. These large marine mammals, sometimes called "sea cows," usually stay close to shore as they migrate up and down the coast, feeding on plants as they slowly move through the water. These gentle giants may weigh up to a ton. The manatee is an endangered species with an estimated total population of 1,200 in Florida. The biggest threats to their safety are collisions with powerboats.

The trees' leaves and other organic material associated with the birds and other animals provide large amounts of organic debris that is washed into the ocean to be used as food. The mangroves act as a filter, keeping the water clean but allowing this organic material to feed the life that teems in the sheltered wetlands and marshes.

A multitude of reef animals use these protected estuaries for shelter, food, and as a nursery. Many species of fish—snappers, sea trout, jacks, shrimp, and spiny lobsters—get their chance at life in these protected areas. Other animals found near the shore are a variety of sponges, snook, crabs, oysters, and isolated species of coral. Beyond park boundaries, unprotected and developed shoreline in many areas along the coast has had disastrous consequences for the wildlife and plants that are dependent on clean water and protected habitat. Silt-laden water in disturbed areas covers coral polyps and the reefs die.

### SUGGESTED READING

HOFFMEISTER, JOHN. *Land from the Sea.* Coral Gables, Florida: University of Miami Press, 1974.

ROBYNS, CARLETON RAY AND JOHN DOUGAS. *Atlantic Coast Fishes.* Boston, Massachusetts: Houghton Mifflin Company, 1986.

▲ **Coffee-bean snails attach themselves** to the roots of the red mangrove tree. They feed on the decaying plant material that falls into the water.

◄ **Elliott Key has a developed trail system** for hikes into the hardwood forest and along the eastern side of the island. Sandy beaches are rare within Biscayne National Park, and most of the shoreline is hard to define as the red mangrove trees reach out into the shallow water. Hiking the islands is best in the winter when the weather is pleasant and the mosquitoes are less numerous.

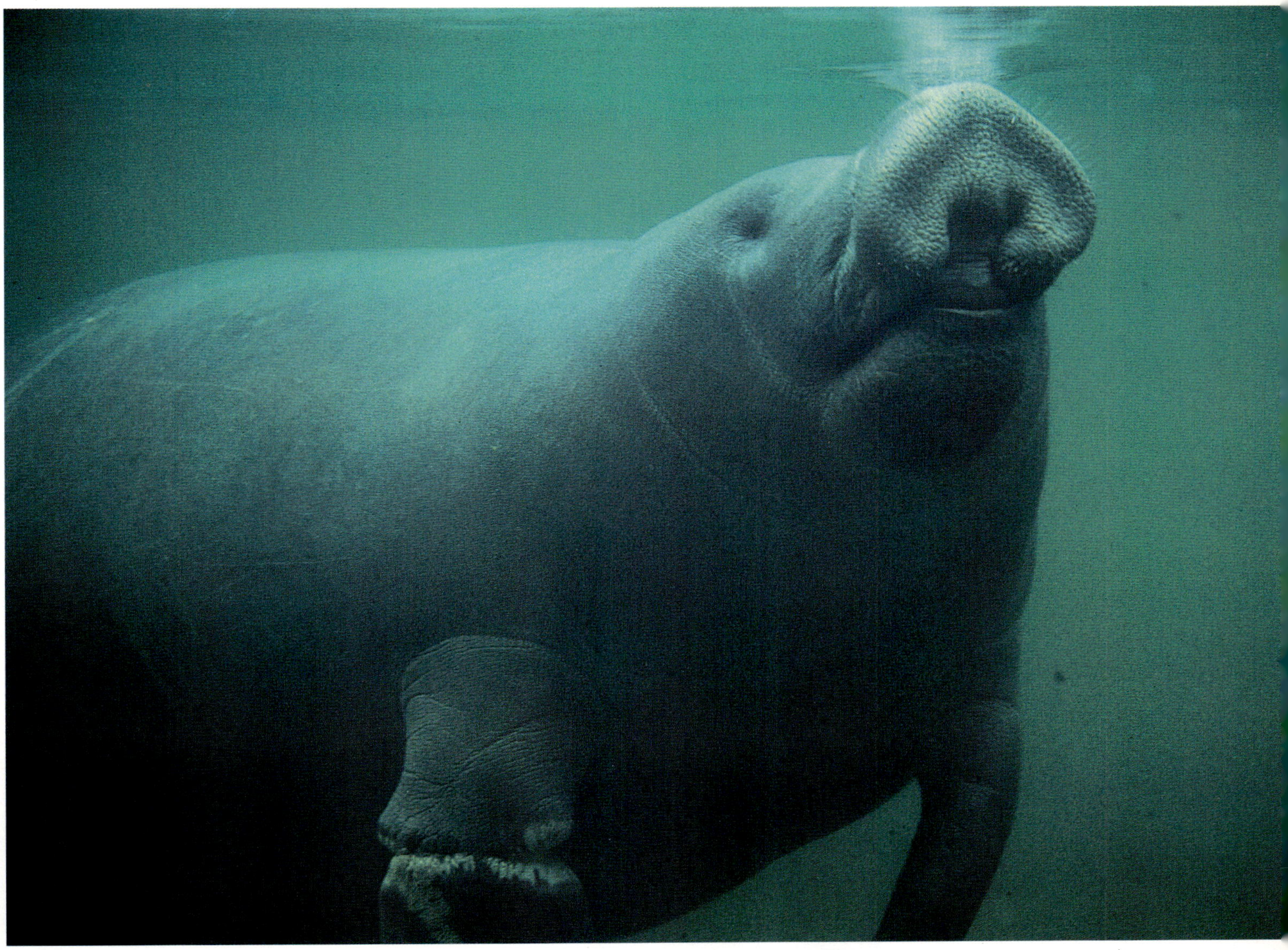

JAMES A. KERN

**The manatee are large** animals found in the park's waters. They are air-breathing mammals, commonly seen in pairs or groups. They have a large, flat tail, no back legs, and their front legs are modified into flippers for swimming. They feed on the grasses, such as turtle grass, found in the water. These animals are in danger of becoming extinct. It is estimated that there are only 1,200 left in Florida. These gentle, slow-moving animals are often hit by powerboats. Scars from boat props are common on the backs of older manatees.

STEPHEN FRINK

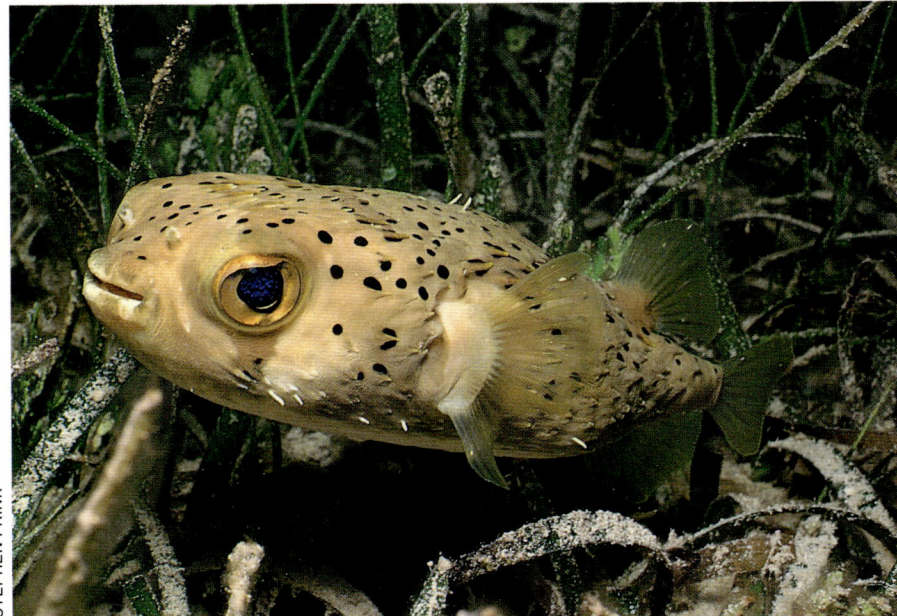

**The pufferfish can enlarge its body by taking in water.** *They are noted world-wide for being poisonous when eaten by humans. Abundant turtle grass provides protection for small animals and food for the manatee.*

◀ **The wood** stork—the only American stork—is seen along the mangroves. This wading bird, once common, is becoming rare. It eats large numbers of fish which it stalks, catching them as it sweeps its bill through the water.

**The anhinga is** ▶ usually found in fresh water along the coast, the park's western boundary. This graceful swimming and diving bird often appears to run on the water on takeoff, building up speed to fly. It is commonly seen perched on a tree with wings spread out to dry in the sun.

▲ **The willet, with its pointed wings and** contrasting black and white wing stripe is easily identified in flight. It is a common sight in Biscayne. This shore bird prefers saltwater marshes.

**The osprey, often called a fish hawk,** ▲ has a wing span of up to four and one-half feet. Feeding almost exclusively on fish, it hovers over the water until it spots its meal, then dives down to snatch it out of the water with its claws.

▲ **This fish-catching royal tern feeds only in salt** water—usually offshore.

◄ **The yellow-crowned night heron feeds on** fish by catching them in its bill, then flipping them in the air, catching and swallowing them head first.

*Sponges are simple animals in a variety of sizes. Unlike most animals that react when touched, the sponge just sits there unaware of human presence. They are a mass of cells on an internal skeleton, having no nervous system, no eyes, and no nose or mouth.*

## Biscayne Bay

Between the tree-lined coast and the islands is Biscayne Bay. This is a wide, shallow bay of sparkling, crystal-clear water. It is protected from the ocean by the barrier islands and continues to provide a protected environment for the animals, from the shore estuaries out into the dense beds of turtle grass and patches of algae on the bottom. Lobsters are protected in the bay as they mature and gradually move out into deeper water.

Sponges of many shapes and forms abound in Biscayne Bay. Sponges are simple animals. They grow attached to the bottom of the bay in a variety of sizes, shapes, and colors. Unlike most animals that react when touched, the sponge just sits there unaware of human presence. They are a mass of cells on an internal skeleton, having no nervous system, no eyes, and no nose or mouth.

Sponges are full of thousands of small holes.

▼ **Access to Biscayne's offshore areas is** by boat from several coastal marinas, such as Homestead Bayfront Park. Throughout the year, boaters pour into the park from these marinas.

**The underwater park is full of** ▷ intriguing forms and shapes. The diver's light casts an eerie glow on a large sponge and associated marine life.

WAYNE LANDRUM

> *Biscayne Bay and the barrier islands play an important role in protecting the mainland against these destructive storms.*
> *The outer reefs are the first barrier to a hurricane, slowing the wave action.*

They feed on plankton by creating a current, drawing plankton into the holes with hairlike appendages. These sponges perform a unique service for the bay and the reefs as each one will filter several quarts of water every day, removing very small particles (even bacteria) that are suspended in the sea. Eighty percent of the material they feed on and filter is too small for other filter feeders to catch.

Individual sponge cells act independently, but have an unusual ability to reform. Many years ago, a sponge was pulverized and filtered until all the individual cells were separated in a dish. Within one day the cells made their way back together, forming a sponge shape like the original!

Sponges become communities—allowing many small animals, such as small fish, shrimp, and brittle stars, to use them for protection.

### HURRICANES

Hurricanes have hit the Florida coast 50 times in the last 100 years. Biscayne Bay and the barrier islands play an important role in protecting the mainland against these destructive storms. The outer reefs are the first barrier to a hurricane, slowing the wave action. These reefs can be decimated by strong winds and tidal surges. The second barrier is the islands. The sturdy mangroves and hardwood forests provide an excellent buffer. The shallow bay also tends to dissipate any storm action.

Florida is in a hurricane zone and has suffered many lost lives and property damage over the years. The hurricane season is June through November. In 1935, a hurricane killed 1,000 persons in the upper keys. Hopefully, with today's advance warnings and preparation, the loss of life will be minimized should a hurricane strike.

### SUGGESTED READING

BROOKFIELD, CHARLES M. and OLIVER GRISSOLD. *They All Called it Tropical.* Miami, Florida: Historical Association of Southern Florida, 1985.

MUNROE, RALPH MIDDLETON and VINCENT GILPIN. *The Commodore's Story.* Miami, Florida: Historical Association of Southern Florida, 1985.

▲ **The cowfish has a funny-shaped face and a** small mouth. This fish feeds on plants along the bottom.

▲ **The beautiful flame scallop is a filter** feeder, not commonly seen in the park. The scallop is a free swimmer.

▲ **There are many species of the colorful, sponge-eating angelfish in the park. The** young have a separate color phase from the adults. Shown here are French angelfish—the one top right is a juvenile, and the one on the left is an adult.

◄ **The small, colorful shrimp is one of the** cleaner shrimp. Fish will come to these shrimp for the removal of parasites, fungi, and dead skin.

▲ **Goatfish grow to about 15 inches long.** These pretty fish probe the sandy bottom with their whiskers in search of food.

◄ **Plume worms are some of the** most colorful creatures of the reef. The feathery extensions filter and capture food.

*When the Spaniards arrived,
the Tequestas were using pottery, dugout canoes,
and hunting with bows and arrows.
A primary food source was the conch
—evidenced by the thousands of shells littering the middens.*

# People at Biscayne

The earliest known residents of what is now the Biscayne National Park were the Tequesta Indians. They lived by fishing and hunting for sea turtles, sharks, sailfish, stingrays, and sea mammals. The manatee, presently an endangered species, was hunted for food as was the porpoise. Non-marine animals taken were deer and freshwater turtles. The Tequesta also gathered native plants, such as the prickly pear, sea grape, and coco plum.

When the Spaniards arrived, the Tequestas were using pottery, dugout canoes, and hunting with bows and arrows. Marine shells were used for tools, decoration, and trade items. Their refuse and trash built up middens (mounds) of shells and animal bones at camp and village sites. Several of these are located on the islands. A primary food source was the conch—evidenced by the thousands of shells littering the middens. By 1763, due to diseases brought to the new world by Europeans and raids by other Indians and the Spanish, the Tequesta were all but wiped out.

### THE SPANISH

Juan Ponce de Leon landed on the coast of Florida in 1513 with three small sailing vessels, claiming the land for Spain. He sailed south along the coast, stopping at a Tequesta village on the Miami River, just outside what is now the park boundary. He then sailed to the end of the Florida Keys and up into the Gulf of Mexico. He was driven off land by hostile Indians and returned to Biscayne Bay for fresh water, abandoning his attempt to settle in Florida.

After Spain conquered the Aztecs in Mexico, gold- and silver-laden ships began to sail between Florida and Cuba through the Straits of Florida. Ponce de Leon returned to Florida in 1521 to start a colony but again was attacked and driven off, suffering an arrow wound in the leg and later dying from the injury. The Spanish eventually established control of Florida and maintained it for 200 years.

### PIRATES

The Spanish treasure fleets carried a steady stream of riches back to Spain. It was not long before British, French, and Dutch pirate ships

▲ **The hawksbill, one of the smaller marine** turtles, may reach 160 pounds, but large individuals are rare. This turtle eats algae, sponges, and soft corals. It seldom comes ashore except to lay eggs.

STEPHEN FRINK

*The larger islands of the park start at Sands Key and stretch south in a line, forming the northern extension of the Florida Keys. These islands, once inhabited by Indians and pirates, were later developed into farms for pineapples, tomatoes, and limes.*

began to prowl the area off the Florida coast to rob the fleets. Thus began an era of violence sparked by greed. The Spanish took the riches from the Americas in exchange for disease and death—and the rest of the world took from the Spaniards. Much of this activity occurred in the vicinity of today's park. Legends tell of a pirate named Black Caesar operating out of a creek near Adams Key. He supposedly hid in the creek out of sight and waited for his victim ships to appear off the island.

Pirates were not the only danger lurking along the keys. The shallow reefs were deadly to ships that ran aground in the unmarked and poorly charted area. From the time of the Spanish fleets to modern times, many ships went to the bottom in or near the present park.

## WRECKERS

Once the pirates were finally driven out a new business emerged—people, known as wreckers, began to salvage the goods from wrecked ships. The curved channel through the Florida Straits, with the shallow reefs on one side and the rocky shores of Cuba on the other, brought busi-

*The sea grape is a common tree of the islands and mainland. It was a food source for the early Indians in the area.*

> *Wreckers were given a license to operate, and the first one to reach a wreck had control of the site. Many of the first residents of Elliott Key were in the wrecking business.*

ness to the wreckers several times a year. A graveyard of ships began to litter the bottom.

The Indians were good swimmers and were the first to take advantage of the wrecked Spanish ships. After the English took over the area and pirating ceased, traffic increased and a great number of ships sank on the reefs. Wrecking became big business during the 1800s, with salvage ports developed all along the Florida Keys. Wreckers were given a license to operate, and the first one to reach a wreck had control of the site. Others arriving on the scene were hired by the "wrecking master." Many of the first residents of Elliott Key were in the wrecking business.

By the turn of the twentieth century, the United States government installed lights and navigation aids along the outside of the reefs so wrecking was no longer profitable. However, even today, many ships and boats run aground on these reefs.

Wreckers and other local residents turned to other methods of making a living. Sea turtles were common in Biscayne Bay at that time, feeding on the sea grasses on the shallow bay bottom. It was common to have as many as 20 turtles, each weighing up to 300 pounds or more, taken on a single day by turtle hunters. This greatly depleted their numbers. In the late 1960s, the turtles were protected in the United States, and most are now on the Endangered Species list.

Sponging became a business in the bay in the 1800s. As many as 150 spongers' boats could be counted working in the bay, hooking the sponges off the bottom with a long pole. In 1905, the sponges were affected by a disease, and in the early 1940s the combination of disease and overharvesting ended most of the sponging. Today, there is some harvesting of sponges, and due to a limited supply worldwide, the price of natural sponges has greatly increased.

### FARMERS

The larger barrier islands in the park were eventually settled. Elliott and Old Rhodes keys were suitable for growing crops. Even though the ground was hard, pineapples, tomatoes, and limes were cultivated. Farming these crops became a profitable venture when the railroad was extended down the coast to Miami in 1886 and, later, all the way to Key West. Working in the fields was hard work, using a pickaxe to dig into the hard limestone while, at the same time, fighting off the mosquitoes.

▲ **The conch has a protective shell and** moves about slowly by means of a large foot. When the animal is approached, or feels threatened, it will retract into the shell and the foot will be pulled into its protective hard disk.

In 1906, a hurricane hit the islands, destroying the pineapple crop and covering the soil with salt. Competition from Cuban and Hawaiian pineapples eventually made it impractical to raise them on the islands, and the demand for limes dropped with prohibition.

### ESTABLISHING A PARK

Most of the people moved off the islands, as pressure to develop the islands was stymied by lack of access to them. However, as late as 1960, plans were proposed to build causeways and roads connecting the islands from Key Biscayne to

▲ **Shipwrecks have** been a common occurrence since the Spaniards first sailed along the Florida coast. Ships often were driven into the reefs by storms or hurricanes in these poorly charted waters. Recent history of this shallow water continues to take its toll on boats and the reefs due to careless operators and poor navigation.

**The corals begin** ▷ to reclaim the bottom on and around the Lugana shipwreck. Schools of fish are attracted to the shelter provided by the ship.

*T*he monument was enlarged in 1974, and again in 1980 to its present size of 181,500 acres and established by an Act of Congress as Biscayne National Park.

---

Key Largo. Dade County almost built the road and causeway, but decided the property owners should pay for it. The city of Islandia was formed with the idea of making the islands into an ocean resort, but many people were alarmed at the prospect of turning the area into another urban beachfront community.

The concept became a raging debate and Stuart Udall, then Secretary of the Interior, directed studies on the area's potential as a national park. Subsequently, President Lyndon B. Johnson set aside the area as a National Monument in 1968. The monument was enlarged in 1974, and again in 1980 to its present size of 181,500 acres and established by an Act of Congress as Biscayne National Park.

Today the park attracts thousands of visitors each year. A concessioner runs glass-bottom boats out to the reefs for sightseeing, snorkeling, and diving. These boats leave from the park headquarters area at Convoy Point. Adams Key and Elliott Key have small visitor centers, hiking trails, and boat docks. Boca Chita is a beautiful small island with a protected harbor. From here one can watch the sun rise from the sea in the morning and set spectacularly in the waters of Biscayne Bay. A beautiful view of the Miami skyline may also be seen from Boca Chita, reminding us that this seemingly remote paradise is only a few miles from a major metropolis.

Park rangers live on Elliott Key and Adams Key. The only other persons living in the park are long-time residents Mrs. Virginia Tannehill and "Sir" Lancelot Jones.

### SUGGESTED READING

MILANICH, JERALD T. and CHARLES H. FAIRBANKS. *Florida Archaeology*. Gainesville, Florida: Academic Press, 1983.

NIEDHAUK, CHARLOTTE ARPIN. *Charlotte's Story*. Pompano Beach, Florida: Exposition Press of Florida, Inc., 1973.

OPPEL, FRANK and TONY MEISEL, ed. *Tales of Old Florida*. Secaucus, New Jersey: Castle, 1987.

TEBEAU, CHARLTON W. *A History of Florida*. Coral Gables, Florida: University of Miami Press, 1971.

▲ **When Biscayne National Park was** established, fishing was allowed to continue according to Florida state law. Many thousands of people come into the park to fish, either from the shore or by boating out around the islands. The park waters extend several miles offshore to a depth of 60 feet.

▲ **Windsurfing is a popular** pastime on Biscayne Bay—but the wind is always a fickle partner.

◄ **One of the concession boats on its** way to the coral reefs. The boats leave the park headquarters daily for trips to the reefs and up to ten miles off the coast and east of the island chain.

▲ **Arriving by private or concessioner boats, campers can go ashore at Boca Chita and** Elliott keys. These islands offer pleasant relief from the congestion of the nearby urban area, but summer camping is discouraged by tremendous populations of mosquitoes.

▲ **Raccoons are the most commonly** seen mammal living on the islands. They have been accustomed to people and are very bold, but do not feed them!

▲ **Sailing is also a popular sport on Biscayne Bay. Gentle winds** and warm, sunny weather encourage this activity.

▲ **Biscayne National Park is one of the very popular fishing areas for the exciting** bonefish. They thrive in the shallow waters and are considered an unequalled sport fish. Bonefish are strong and fast, and feed on crabs and clams.

▲ **The Key Largo wood rat is an** endangered species, living only in mature, tropical hardwood hammocks. They build large stick houses.

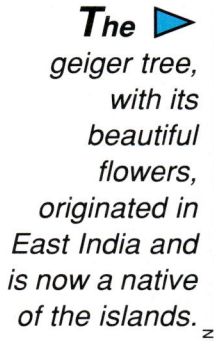

**The** ▷ geiger tree, with its beautiful flowers, originated in East India and is now a native of the islands.

▲ **The Shaus butterfly is a rare** swallowtail. A protected species, it eats the leaves of the torchwood tree.

◁ **Commonly found on Sands Key, the prickly-**pear cacti have beautiful flowers, and the fruit is edible.

**Elliott Key** ▷ harbor, located on the bay side of the island, is protected and has a visitor center. Nearby is a primitive campground with hiking trails and cold-water showers.

◀ **Boca Chita** Key, in the northern part of the park, has a beautiful harbor. Once owned by the Honeywell family, this picturesque island has an ornamental 65-foot lighthouse constructed by them in the 1930s. It was lighted only once, then declared a hazard to navigation by the U.S. Coast Guard. Shallow waters around all the islands are constantly impacted by boats that run aground, leaving prop scars that are plainly visible.

**Adams Key** ▶ was once developed as the Cocolobo Club hideaway for the rich and famous. Presidents Harding, Roosevelt, Johnson, and Nixon stayed at this resort. Today park rangers live on the island.

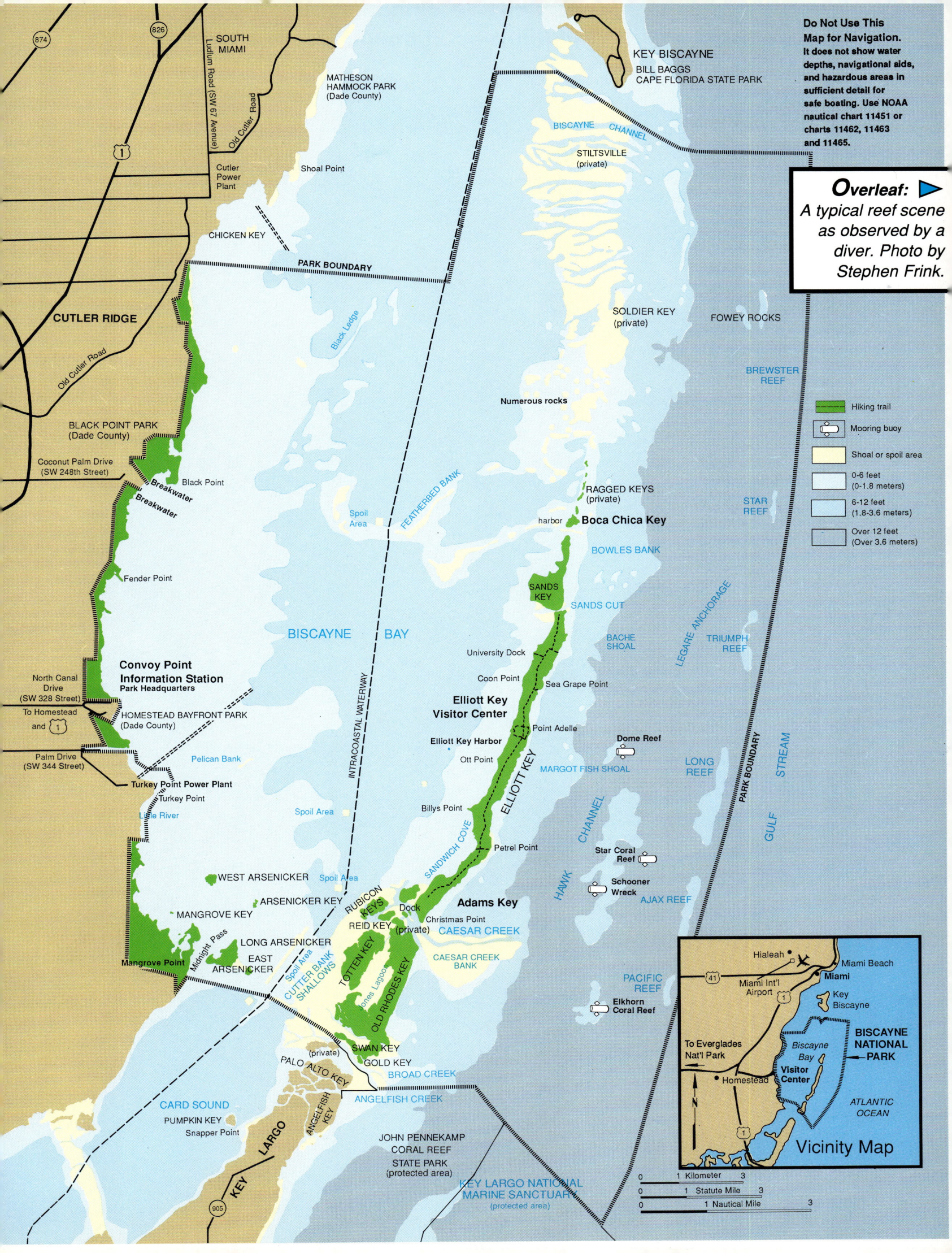

# Biscayne National Park Map

**Do Not Use This Map for Navigation.** It does not show water depths, navigational aids, and hazardous areas in sufficient detail for safe boating. Use NOAA nautical chart 11451 or charts 11462, 11463 and 11465.

**Overleaf:** ▶
*A typical reef scene as observed by a diver. Photo by Stephen Frink.*

## Legend
- Hiking trail
- Mooring buoy
- Shoal or spoil area
- 0–6 feet (0–1.8 meters)
- 6–12 feet (1.8–3.6 meters)
- Over 12 feet (Over 3.6 meters)

## Labels on Main Map

**Mainland / West side (top to bottom):**
- SOUTH MIAMI
- Ludlum Road (SW 67 Avenue)
- Old Cutler Road
- MATHESON HAMMOCK PARK (Dade County)
- Cutler Power Plant
- CUTLER RIDGE
- Shoal Point
- CHICKEN KEY
- PARK BOUNDARY
- BLACK POINT PARK (Dade County)
- Coconut Palm Drive (SW 248th Street)
- Black Point
- Breakwater
- Breakwater
- Fender Point
- Convoy Point Information Station — Park Headquarters
- North Canal Drive (SW 328 Street)
- To Homestead and 1
- HOMESTEAD BAYFRONT PARK (Dade County)
- Palm Drive (SW 344 Street)
- Pelican Bank
- Turkey Point Power Plant
- Turkey Point
- Little River
- Spoil Area
- WEST ARSENICKER
- ARSENICKER KEY
- MANGROVE KEY
- LONG ARSENICKER
- EAST ARSENICKER
- Mangrove Point
- Midnight Pass
- CUTTER BANK SHALLOWS
- RUBICON KEYS
- REID KEY
- TOTTEN KEY
- OLD RHODES KEY
- SWAN KEY (private)
- GOLD KEY
- PALO ALTO KEY
- CARD SOUND
- PUMPKIN KEY
- Snapper Point
- ANGELFISH KEY
- KEY LARGO
- JOHN PENNEKAMP CORAL REEF STATE PARK (protected area)
- KEY LARGO NATIONAL MARINE SANCTUARY (protected area)

**Bay / Ocean side (top to bottom):**
- KEY BISCAYNE — BILL BAGGS CAPE FLORIDA STATE PARK
- BISCAYNE CHANNEL
- STILTSVILLE (private)
- Black Ledge
- SOLDIER KEY (private)
- FOWEY ROCKS
- BREWSTER REEF
- Numerous rocks
- FEATHERBED BANK
- Spoil Area
- RAGGED KEYS (private)
- STAR REEF
- harbor — Boca Chica Key
- BOWLES BANK
- SANDS KEY
- SANDS CUT
- BISCAYNE BAY
- INTRACOASTAL WATERWAY
- BACHE SHOAL
- LEGARE ANCHORAGE
- TRIUMPH REEF
- University Dock
- Coon Point
- Sea Grape Point
- Elliott Key Visitor Center
- Point Adelle
- Elliott Key Harbor
- Dome Reef
- Ott Point
- ELLIOTT KEY
- MARGOT FISH SHOAL
- LONG REEF
- Billys Point
- PARK BOUNDARY
- SANDWICH COVE
- Petrel Point
- HAWK CHANNEL
- Star Coral Reef
- Schooner Wreck
- AJAX REEF
- GULF STREAM
- Dock
- Christmas Point
- Adams Key (private)
- CAESAR CREEK
- CAESAR CREEK BANK
- Jones Lagoon
- PACIFIC REEF
- BROAD CREEK
- ANGELFISH CREEK
- Elkhorn Coral Reef

## Vicinity Map
- Hialeah
- 41
- Miami Beach
- Miami Int'l Airport
- Miami
- 1
- Key Biscayne
- To Everglades Nat'l Park
- Biscayne Bay
- Homestead
- Visitor Center
- BISCAYNE NATIONAL PARK
- ATLANTIC OCEAN
- 1

## Scale
- 1 Kilometer — 3
- 1 Statute Mile — 3
- 1 Nautical Mile — 3

# Man on the Edge

Biscayne is a fragile environment. The coral reefs here are growing on the very northern edge of their range. Slight temperature changes or decreases in water quality could kill the reefs. Should the reef system not be protected, the communities of plants and animals that are dependent on it for food and shelter could not survive.

There are many threats to this paradise. The living reef system is the only one in the world located so close to such a large population, which creates pressures on the system. The city of Miami and the outlying communities are crowding up against the park. These people, with easy access to the park, pour into it for boating, water skiing, fishing and diving, and just to escape from the urban environment. The islands, mostly uninhabited, are a world away from the bustling city.

When one looks beyond the sparkling waters of Biscayne Bay, the urban environment is highly visible. The city of Miami, with its skyscrapers, appears to rise from the water when viewed from the islands.

All these pressures put demands on this natural environment. We must watch closely any changes taking place that could erode the value of the park or put its systems in jeopardy. Our role at Biscayne must be to direct the uses that occur here, and encourage the park's neighbors and visitors to participate in the protection of this fragile system. With understanding, the unique value of Biscayne National Park can remain a healthy ecological system, and a haven for the plants and animals that depend on its existence.

*The Miami skyline from Boca Chita.*

**Books in the Story Behind the Scenery series:** Acadia, Alcatraz Island, Arches, Biscayne, Blue Ridge Parkway, Bryce Canyon, Canyon de Chelly, Canyonlands, Cape Cod, Capitol Reef, Channel Islands, Civil War Parks, Colonial, Crater Lake, Death Valley, Denali, Dinosaur, Everglades, Fort Clatsop, Gettysburg, Glacier, Glen Canyon-Lake Powell, Grand Canyon, Grand Canyon-North Rim, Grand Teton, Great Smoky Mountains, Haleakala, Hawaii Volcanoes, Independence, Lake Mead-Hoover Dam, Lassen Volcanic, Lincoln Parks, Mount Rainier, Mount Rushmore, Mount St. Helens, National Park Service, National Seashores, North Cascades, Olympic, Petrified Forest, Redwood, Rocky Mountain, Scotty's Castle, Sequoia-Kings Canyon, Shenandoah, Statue of Liberty, Theodore Roosevelt, Virgin Islands, Yellowstone, Yosemite, Zion.
**NEW: in pictures—The Continuing Story:** Bryce Canyon, Death Valley, Everglades, Grand Canyon, Sequoia-Kings Canyon, Yellowstone, Zion.

**Published by KC Publications • Box 14883 • Las Vegas, NV 89114**

▶ **Inside back cover:** A diver safely passes over the elkhorn coral. Photo by Stephen Frink.

▶ **Back cover:** The gentle, slow-moving manatee have been here for thousands of years. Photo by Tom Campbell.

Printed by Dong-A Printing and Publishing, Seoul, Korea
Color Separations by Kedia/Kwangyangsa Co., Ltd.